CONTENTS

C000108416

For pattern inquiries, please visit: www.go-crafty.com

Sweet DREAMS

YOU'LL NEED

YARN:  5¼oz/150g, 410yd/375m of any sport weight cotton in light pink (MC)

3½oz/100g, 280yd/256m in light green (A), coral (B), and orange (D)

1¾oz/50g, 140yd/128m in yellow (C)

HOOK: Size E/4 (3.5mm) crochet hook *or size to obtain gauge*

FINISHED MEASUREMENTS

Approx 25"x 28"/63.5cm x 71cm

GAUGE

One square to 3"/7.5cm using size E/4 (3.5mm) crochet hook.
Take time to check gauge.

STITCH GLOSSARY

CL (cluster st)
Work 3 dc in the same ch-sp or st as stated in the edging directions.

BASIC GRANNY SQUARE

Note See placement diagram for color order of the first 3 rnds.
With first color, ch 4. Join ch with a sl st forming a ring.
Rnd 1 (RS) Ch 5 (counts as 1 dc and ch 2), [dc in ring, ch 2] 7 times. Join rnd with a sl st in 3rd ch of ch-5. Fasten off.
Rnd 2 Join 2nd color with a sl st in any ch-2 sp. Ch 3 (always counts as 1 dc), work 2 dc in same sp, ch 2, [work 3 dc in next ch-2 sp, ch 2] 7 times. Join rnd with a sl st in 3rd ch of ch-3. Fasten off. **Rnd 3** Join 3rd color with a sl st in any ch-2 sp. Ch 3, work (2 dc, ch 1, 3 dc) in same sp, ch 1, [work (3 dc, ch 1, 3 dc) in next ch-2 sp, ch 1] 7 times. Join rnd with a sl st in 3rd ch of ch-3. Fasten off.
Rnd 4 Join MC with a sl st in any ch-1 sp. Ch 3, work (2 dc, ch 1, 3 dc) in same sp (first corner made), ch 1, *[sc in next ch-1 sp, ch 2] twice, sc in next ch-1 sp, ch 1, work (3 dc, ch 1, 3 dc) in next ch-1 sp, ch 1; rep from * around, end [sc in next ch-1 sp, ch 2] twice, sc in next ch-1 sp, ch 1. Join rnd with a sl st in 3rd ch of ch-3. Fasten off.
Make 56 squares foll placement diagram for colorways.

FINISHING

Sew squares tog foll placement diagram.

EDGING

Note On rnd 1, you will not only be working into the 4 outer corner ch-1 sps of the corner squares to form new corners, but as you work across each side edge of the blanket, you will also be working into the inner corner ch-1 sps of squares at the joined seams.
Rnd 1 (RS) Join MC with a sl st in any outer corner ch-1 sp. Ch 5 (counts as 1 hdc and ch 3), hdc in same sp (first corner made), ** *hdc in next ch-1 sp, ch 2, [hdc in next ch-2 sp, ch 2] twice, hdc in next ch-1 sp, ch 2, hdc in opposite corner ch-1 sp of same square, ch 2, sk joined seam, hdc in corner ch-1 sp of next square, ch 2; rep from * to next outer corner ch-1 sp, work (hdc, ch 3, hdc) in sp; rep from ** around. Join rnd with a sl st in 2nd ch of ch-5. Fasten off. **Rnd 2** Join A with a sl st in any corner ch-3 sp. Ch 3 (counts as 1 dc), work 4 dc in same sp (first corner made), ch 2, ** *CL in next ch-2 sp, ch 2, sk next ch-2 sp; rep from * to next corner ch-3 sp, work 5 dc in sp, ch 2; rep from ** around. Join rnd with a sl st in 3rd ch of ch-3. Fasten off.
Rnd 3 Join C with a sl st in first dc of any 5-dc corner. Ch 3 (counts as 1 dc), work 2 dc in same st, ch 1, work 5dc in 3rd of same corner, ch 1, work CL in 5th dc of same corner, ch 2, ** *CL in 2nd dc of next CL, ch 2; rep from * to next 5-dc corner, work (CL in first dc of corner, ch 1, 5 dc in 3rd dc, ch 1, CL in 5th dc) ch 2; rep from ** around. Join rnd with a sl st in 3rd ch of ch-3. Fasten off. **Rnd 4** Join B with a sl st in first dc of any 5-dc corner. Ch 3 (counts as 1 dc), work 2 dc in same st, ch 1, work 3dc in 3rd dc of same corner, ch 1, work CL in 5th dc of same corner, ch 2, ** *CL in 2nd dc of next CL, ch 2; rep from * to next 5-dc corner, work (CL in first dc of corner, ch 1, CL in 3rd dc, ch 1, CL in 5th dc) ch 2; rep from ** around. Join rnd with a sl st in 3rd ch of ch-3. Fasten off.
Rnd 5 Join D with a sl st in 2nd dc of any corner CL. Ch 7 (counts as 1 dc and ch 4), sl st in 4th ch from hook (picot made), dc in same st, ch 2, *sc in next ch-sp, dc in 2nd dc of next cluster, ch 4, sl st in 4th ch from hook, dc in same st, ch 2; rep from * around. Join rnd with a sl st in 3rd ch of ch-7. Fasten off.

PLACEMENT DIAGRAM

C, B, A	A, C, B	D, A, C	B, MC, A	D, MC, B	C, B, A	B, MC, B	A, D, A
A, C, B	C, A, D	B, MC, A	C, A, B	A, D, A	MC, D, C	A, D, A	MC, C, B
B, MC, A	MC, D, B	C, A, D	B, MC, A	C, B, D	D, A, B	B, MC, D	C, B, A
C, A, D	D, A, C	A, C, B	MC, D, C	D, MC, B	B, C, A	MC, C, B	B, A, C
D, A, B	B, MC, A	C, A, D	D, A, B	A, C, A	MC, D, B	C, D, A	D, B, D
MC, D, C	A, B, D	MC, D, B	A, B, A	MC, C, B	C, B, A	MC, D, C	B, MC, A
B, C, A	D, MC, B	B, C, A	C, B, D	D, A, C	MC, D, B	C, B, A	A, C, D

Color Key
Lt pink (MC)
Lt Green (A)
Coral (B)
Yellow (C)
Orange (D)

Bright IDEA

Jose Santa

YOU'LL NEED

YARN:  5¼oz/150g, 570yd/520m of any fingering weight wool yarn in red (MC)

1¾oz/50g, 189yd/175m in pink (A), coral (B), orange (C), and purple (D)

HOOK: Size E/4 (3.5mm) crochet hook *or size to obtain gauge*

FINISHED MEASUREMENTS

Approx 20"x 26"/50.5cm x 66cm

GAUGE

One square to 3¼"/8.5cm using size E/4 (3.5mm) crochet hook.
Take time to check gauge

BASIC GRANNY SQUARE

With first color, ch 5. Join with sl st to first ch to form ring.

Rnd 1 Ch 3, work 2 dc in ring, [ch 3, work 3 dc in ring] 3 times, ch 3, join with sl st to top of ch-3 at beg of rnd. Fasten off.

Rnd 2 Join 2nd color in any space made by ch-3. Ch 3, 1 dc in same space, [dc in each of next 3 dc, in next ch-3 sp work 2 dc, ch 3 and 2 dc] 3 times, dc in each of next 3 dc, 2 dc in same sp at beg of rnd. Fasten off.

Rnd 3 Join 3rd color in any space made by ch-3. Ch 3, 1 dc in same space, [dc in each of next 7 dc, in next ch-3 sp work 2 dc, ch 3 and 2 dc] 3 times, dc in each of next 7 dc, 2 dc in same sp at

beg of rnd. Fasten off.

Rnd 4 With MC, rep rnd 3, working 11 dc between corners.

Make squares following placement diagram for colorways.

FINISHING

With MC, crochet squares tog foll placement diagram.

EDGING

With RS facing and MC, work as foll: join MC to any corner ch-3 space, work 3 dc in same space, *ch 3, sl st in 3nd ch, sk 3 dc, work 3 dc in next dc; rep from * to next corner, work 6 dc in corner ch-3 sp, cont in this way around entire blanket. Join and fasten off.

PLACEMENT DIAGRAM

B, D, A	A, B, C	MC, C, D	C, D, A	D, C, B	A, C, D
D, B, C	B, A, D	D, B, A	MC, A, C	C, B, D	B, D, C
C, A, D	C, A, B	B, C, D	A, C, B	MC, D, A	C, A, D
A, D, B	MC, C, D	D, A, C	D, B, A	A, C, D	D, B, A
D, B, A	D, C, B	B, A, D	MC, B, C	C, D, A	A, D, B
C, A, D	MC, D, A	C, A, B	B, C, D	D, A, C	C, A, D
B, D, C	C, B, D	MC, A, C	D, B, A	B, A, D	D, B, C
A, C, D	D, C, B	C, D, A	MC, C, D	A, B, C	B, D, A

Color Key
Red (MC)
Pink (A)
Coral (B)
Orange (C)
Purple (D)

Cradle COMFORT

YOU'LL NEED

YARN:  3½oz/100g, 280yd/256m of any sport weight cotton in light blue (A), yellow (B), light teal (C) and light green (D)

HOOK: Size E/4 (3.5mm) crochet hook *or size to obtain gauge*

FINISHED MEASUREMENTS
Approx 23½"x 27"/59.5cm x 68.5cm

GAUGE
35 sts and 18 rows to 5"/12.5cm over pat st using size E/4 (3.5mm) crochet hook.
Take time to check gauge.

NOTES
1 When changing colors on a dc row, draw new color through last 2 lps on hook to complete last dc.
2 When changing colors on a sc row, draw new color through 2 lps on hook to complete last sc.

BLANKET
With A, ch 171.
Row 1 (WS) Dc in 4th ch from hook, dc in next 6 ch, *work 3 dc in next ch, dc in next 7 ch, sk next 2 ch, dc in next 7 ch; rep from * across, end work 3 dc in next ch, dc in last 7 ch. Ch 3, turn. Cont to work through back lps only. **Row 2** Sk first st, *dc in next 7 sts, work 3 dc in next st, dc in next 7 sts, sk next 2 sts; rep from *, end dc in next 7 sts, work 3 dc in next st, dc in next 6 sts, sk next st, dc in last st. Join B, ch 1, turn. **Rows 3-6** Sk first st, *sc in next 7 sts, work 3 sc in next st, sc in next 7 sts, sk next 2 sts; rep from * end sc in next 7 sts, work 3 sc in next st, sc in next 6 sts, sk next st, sc in last st. Ch 1, turn. After row 6 is completed, join C, ch 3, turn. **Rows 7 and 8** Rep row 2. After row 8 is completed, join D, ch 1, turn. **Rows 9-12** Rep row 3. After row 12 is completed, join A, ch 3, turn. **Rows 13 and 14** Rep row 2. After row 14 is completed, join B, ch 1, turn. Rep rows 3-14 for pat st and stripe pat. Work even until piece measures 27"/68.5cm from beg, end with row 14. Fasten off.

FINISHING
Block lightly.

Forget-Me-Not THROW

YOU'LL NEED

YARN:  16oz/452g, 900yd/824m of any worsted weight, variegated, superwash wool

HOOK: Size H/8 (5mm) crochet hook *or size to obtain gauge*

FINISHED MEASUREMENTS
Approx 26" x 36"/66cm x 91.5cm

GAUGE
Small square (first 4 rnds of pattern) to 5"/12.5cm using size H/8 (5mm) hook. *Take time to check gauge.*

SQUARE
(make 26 small and 1 large)
Ch 6, join with sl st to first chain to form a ring.
Rnd 1 Ch 5 (counts as tr, ch 1), [1 tr in ring, ch 1] 15 times. Join with sl st to 4th ch of beg ch-5.
Rnd 2 Sl st in first ch-1 sp, (yo, insert hook in same st, yo and pull up a loop) 3 times, yo and pull through all 7 loops on hook (puff st made), ch 2, *puff st in next ch-1 sp, ch 2; rep from * 14 times more. Join with sl st in top of first puff st.
Rnd 3 Sl st in next ch-2 sp, ch 3, (2 dc, ch 1, 3 dc) in same sp, ch 2, [sc in next ch-2 sp, ch 2] 3 times, *(3 dc, ch 1, 3 dc) in next ch-1 sp, ch 2, [sc in next ch-2 sp, ch 2] 3 times; rep from * twice more. Join with sl st to top of beg ch-3.
Rnd 4 Sl st in next 2 dc and next ch-1 sp, ch 3, (2 dc, ch 1, 3 dc) in same sp, ch 1, [2 dc in next ch-2 sp, ch 1] 4 times, *(3 dc, ch 1, 3 dc) in next corner ch-1 sp, ch 1, [2 dc in next ch-2 sp, ch 1] 4 times, rep from * twice more. Join with sl st to top of beg ch-3.
For small square, fasten off.
For large square, cont to end of square pat as foll:
Rnd 5 Sl st in next 2 dc and next ch-1 sp, ch 3, (2 dc, ch 1, 3 dc) in same sp, [ch 2, *puff st in next ch-1 sp, ch 2; rep from * to next corner, (3 dc, ch 1, 3 dc) in corner ch-1 sp] 3 times, ch 2, work puff st in next ch-1 sp, ch 2 to end of rnd. Join with sl st to top of beg ch-3.
Rnd 6 Sl st in next 2 dc and next ch-1 sp, ch 3, (2 dc, ch 1, 3 dc) in same sp, [ch 1, *2 dc in next ch-2 sp, ch 1; rep from * to next corner, (3 dc, ch 1, 3 dc) in corner ch 1 sp] 3 times, ch 1, work 2 dc in next ch-2 sp, ch 1 to end of rnd. Join with sl st to top of beg ch-3.
Rnds 7–18 Rep rnds 5 and 6 six times. Fasten off.

FINISHING
With right sides tog and working in back loops only, whipstitch squares tog foll the placement diagram.

BORDER
Rnd 1 Join yarn with sl st in any corner ch-1 sp. Ch 1, 3 sc in same sp, *sc in each dc and ch 1 sp across to joining, hdc in joining; rep from * across to next corner, 3 sc in corner, cont around entire afghan with sc in each dc and ch-1 sp, hdc in each joining and 3 sc in each corner ch-1 sp. Join with sl st to first sc. (488 sc).
Rnd 2 *Ch 4, tr in same sc as sl st, skip next 3 sc, sl st in next sc; rep from * around. Fasten off. Weave in ends.

ASSEMBLY DIAGRAM

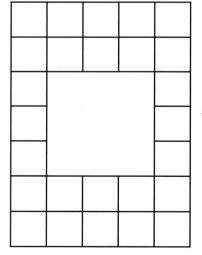

Snuggly Shells BLANKET

YOU'LL NEED

YARN:  8oz/226g, 430yd/395m of any worsted weight wool blend in red (A), gold (B) and variegated red (C)

HOOK: Size G/6 (4mm) crochet hook *or size to obtain gauge*

ADDITIONAL: Yarn needle

FINISHED MEASUREMENTS
Approx 22½"x 31½"/57cm x 80cm

GAUGE
18 sts and 15 rows to 4"/10cm over 7-dc shell pat using size G/6 (4mm) crochet hook.
Take time to check gauge.

BLANKET
With C, ch 116.
Row 1 Work 3 dc in 4th ch from hook, [skip next 3 ch, 1 sc in each of next 7 ch, skip next 3 ch, 7 dc in next ch—shell made] 7 times, skip 3, sc in 7, skip 3, 4dc in last ch. Join A, ch 1, turn.
Row 2 With A, 1 sc in each st across, ending with 1 sc in top of t-ch. Join B, ch 1, turn.
Row 3 With B, 1 sc in each of first 4 sc, *skip 3 sc, shell in next sc, skip 3 sc, 1 sc in each of next 7 sc; rep from * across, ending last rep with skip 3 sc, 1 sc in each of last 4 sc. Join C, ch 3 (counts as 1 dc), turn.
Row 4 With C, 3 dc in first st, *skip next 3 sts, 1 sc in each of next 7 sts, skip next 3 sts, shell in next st; rep from * across, ending last rep with 4 dc in last st. Join A, ch 1, turn.
Rep rows 2–4 in stripe shell pat until piece meas approx 31"/79cm from beg.

FINISHING
Weave and trim ends.

SHELL BORDER
Rnd 1 With C, sc evenly around edge working 3 sc in each corner. Join with sl st to first sc.
Rnd 2 Ch 1, 1 sc in first sc, *skip 1 sc, 5 dc in next sc—shell made, skip 1 sc, 1 sc in next sc; rep from * around working 5-dc shell in each corner, ending last rep with omit 1 sc in next sc. Join with sl st to first sc. Fasten off.
Weave and trim ends.

Jack Deutsch

Light BRIGHT

Jack Deutsch

YOU'LL NEED

YARN: Ⓘ *Microspun* by Lion Brand Yarn Co., 2.5oz/70g, 168yd/154m, acrylic
2 skeins each in #148 Turquoise (A), #109 Royal blue (B), #144 Lilac (C) and #194 Lime (D)

HOOK: Size E/4 (3.5mm) crochet hook *or size to obtain gauge*

ADDITIONAL: Yarn needle

FINISHED MEASUREMENTS

Approx 25"x 27½"/63.5cm x 70cm

GAUGE

34 sts and 16 rows to 5"/12.5cm over pat using size E/4 (3.5mm) crochet hook.
Take time to check gauge.

STITCH GLOSSARY

BL Work through back loops only.

NOTE

Join new color by working in old color to last 2 lps; leaving 6"/15cm tail, complete st by drawing new color through 2 lps and continue with new color.

BLANKET

With A, ch 171.
Row 1 (WS) Work 1 dc in 4th ch from hook, 1 dc in each of next 6 ch, *3 dc in next ch, 1 dc in each of next 7 ch, skip 2 ch, 1 dc in each of next 7 ch; rep from * across end with 3 dc in next ch, 1 dc in each of last 7 ch. Ch 3, turn. Cont to work through BL only.
Row 2 Skip first st, *1 dc in each of next 7 sts, 3 dc in next st, 1 dc in each of next 7 sts, skip 2 sts; rep from *, ending with 1 dc in each of next 7 sts, 3 dc in next st, 1 dc in each of next 6 sts, skip next st, 1 dc in last st. Join B, ch 1, turn.
Rows 3–6 With B, skip first st, *1 sc in each of next 7 sts, 3 sc in next st, 1 sc in each of next 7 sts, skip 2 sts; rep from *, ending with 1 sc in each of next 7 sts, 3 sc in next st, 1 sc in each of next 6 sts, skip next st, 1 sc in last st. Ch 1, turn. After row 6 is completed, join C, ch 3, turn.
Rows 7 and 8 With C, rep row 2. After row 8 is completed, join D, ch 1, turn.
Rows 9–12 With D, rep row 3. After row 12 is completed, join A, ch 3, turn.
Rows 13 and 14 With A, rep row 2. After row 14 is completed, join B, ch 1, turn.
Rep rows 3–14 for stripe pat st until piece measures approx 27½"/70cm from beg, ending with row 14. Fasten off.

FINISHING

Block lightly.

Rainbow of BLOCKS

YOU'LL NEED

YARN:  3½oz/100g, 220yd/200m of any worsted weight cotton/acrylic blend in light blue (A) and ecru (B)

1¾oz/50g, 110yd/100m in pink (C), purple (D), red (E), orange (F), lime green (G), sage green (H), natural (I), and dark blue (J)

HOOK: Size E/4 (3.5mm) crochet hook *or size to obtain gauge*

FINISHED MEASUREMENTS

Approx 33" x 33"/83.5cm x 83.5cm

GAUGE

1 granny square to 4½"/11.5cm using size E/4 (3.5mm) crochet hook.
Take time to check gauge.

NOTES

1 Colors are used randomly and can be placed as desired OR use the placement diagram which shows the color sequence of each square as shown in the photo.

Note that the center square is a solid color, lime green (G). All the other squares change color at the end of every round.

2 When changing colors for each round, dc over yarn tails to hide and then cut. This eliminates weaving in all the tails.

GRANNY SQUARE

Make 49 squares.
Follow the placement diagram for the color sequence of each square or use colors as desired.
Ch 4, join with sl st in first ch to form ring.
Rnd 1 Ch 5, [work 3 dc in ring, ch 2] 3 times, work 2 dc in ring, sl st in 3rd ch of beg ch 5. Fasten off.
Rnd 2 Join new color with sl st into ch-2 sp, ch 5, 3 dc in same sp, *ch 1, (3 dc, ch 2, 3 dc) in next sp; rep from * twice more, ch 1, 2 dc in same sp as beg ch-5, sl st in 3rd ch of ch-5. Fasten off.
Rnd 3 Join new color with sl st into ch-2 sp, ch 5, 3 dc in same sp, *ch 1, 3 dc in next sp, ch 1, (3 dc, ch 2, 3 dc) in next sp; rep from * twice more, ch 1, 3 dc in next sp, ch 1, 2 dc in same sp as beg ch-5, sl st in 3rd ch of ch-5. Fasten off.
Rnd 4 Join new color with sl st into ch-2

sp, ch 5, 3 dc in same sp, *[ch 1, 3 dc in next sp] twice, ch 1, (3 dc, ch 2, 3 dc) in next sp; rep from * twice more, (ch 1, 3 dc in next sp) twice, ch 1, 2 dc in same sp as beg ch-5, sl st in 3rd ch of ch-5. Fasten off.

FINISHING

Block squares to measurement.

JOINING SQUARES

Arrange squares with right sides facing following the placement diagram. With B, single crochet squares together using back loop only of each square. Single crochet all horizontal rows, then vertical rows. Fasten off at the end of each row, except the last seam.
Note Use a sl st when crossing over a previous sc seam.

EDGING

Rnd 1 After seaming the last row, cont with B and work 1 sc in each dc and ch-1 sp, and sl st over seams around border of entire blanket. At each corner, work 3 sc in ch-2 sp. End with sl st in first sc of rnd.
Rnd 2 Join A with sl st, ch 1, sc in same st, sc in each sc around entire blanket, 3 sc in each corner st, end with sl st in beg ch-1.
Rnd 3 Ch 2, work hdc in each sc around, working 3 hdc in each corner st, end with sl st in 2nd chain of beg ch-2.
Rnd 4 Ch 1, work sc in each hdc around, working 3 sc in each corner st.
End with sl st in beg ch-1.

PLACEMENT DIAGRAM

F, A, G, D	H, B, I, C	J, C, D, G	E, B, D, F	D, H, C, A	J, I, E, D	B, F, A, G
C, A, F, B	D, A, C, I	G, E, A, H	J, F, G, I	E, I, D, C	G, E, C, B	C, D, H, E
I, J, F, E	H, C, A, J	I, H, J, F	C, G, F, D	D, A, I, H	B, J, A, I	F, A, G, C
C, B, D, H	E, B, H, I	F, D, E, J	G	G, I, D, A	J, G, E, B	A, J, C, D
I, B, G, J	A, G, J, H	J, B, A, C	H, C, B, E	F, H, A, B	E, A, B, J	D, A, B, F
A, I, G, E	G, C, A, F	E, C, I, A	F, E, D, I	G, J, F, C	F, B, E, A	I, F, B, H
C, J, G, A	F, E, D, G	G, F, I, J	I, E, H, D	C, I, G, F	I, C, D, B	G, D, A, E

COLOR KEY

A Light blue	D Purple	G Lime
B Ecru	E Red	H Sage
C Pink	F Orange	I Natural
		J Dark blue

Lullaby AND GOODNIGHT

YOU'LL NEED

YARN: [4] *Kids* by Red Heart/Coats & Clark, 5oz/141g, 290yd/265m, acrylic

1 skein each in #2845 Blue (A), #2680 Jade (B) and #2652 Lime (C)

HOOK: Crochet hook size K/10½ (6.5mm) *or size to obtain gauge*

FINISHED MEASUREMENTS

Approx 25" x 35"/63.5cm x 89cm

GAUGE

11 ex-sc and 10 rows to 4"/10cm using size K/10½ (6.5mm) crochet hook.
Take time to check gauge.

NOTES

1 The afghan is made in one piece, picking up sts along the sides of rows to create the different directions.
2 Carry the colors not in use along the side of the work and only fasten off when indicated. When working into the sides of the rows, crochet over these strands.

STITCH GLOSSARY

EXTENDED SINGLE CROCHET (ex-sc)
Insert hook into st indicated, yo and draw through, yo and draw through 1 loop on hook, yo and draw through both loops on hook.

AFGHAN

SECTION 1

With A, ch 22.
Row 1 Work 1 ex-sc into 4th ch from hook, 1 ex-sc in next 18 ch. Turn.
Row 2 Ch 2 (counts as first st of this and every row), 1 ex-sc in next 19 sts, working last 2 loops of last st with B. Turn.
Row 3 With B, ch 2, 1 ex-sc in each st. Turn.
Row 4 Ch 2, 1 ex-sc in each st, working last 2 loops of last st with A. Turn.
Row 5 With A, ch 2, ex-sc in each st.

Turn.
Row 6 Ch 2, 1 ex-sc in each st, working last 2 loops of last st with B.
Rows 7–30 Rep rows 3–6 six times. Ch 1 and pull up a long loop of A and leave both yarns attached.

SECTION 2

Attach C at lower edge of fabric on same side as color changes.
Row 1 With C, ch 2, working into sides of each row, work 1 ex-sc in side of next 29 rows, change to A. Fasten off C, turn.
Rows 2 and 3 Rep rows 5 and 6 as of section 1 (29 sts).
Rows 4–19 Rep rows 3–6 of section 1. Change to C at end of row 19 and do not turn. Fasten off colors A and B.

SECTION 3

Rotate piece 90° clockwise.
Row 1 Ch 2, working into side of each row, work 1 ex-sc in side of next 18 rows, working sts into row 30 of section 1, work 1 ex-sc into next 20 sts, change to A, fasten off C, turn.
Rows 2 and 3 Rep rows 5 and 6 of section 1 (38 sts).
Rows 4–27 Rep rows 3–6 of section 1. Change to C at end of row 27 and do not turn. Fasten off A and B.

SECTION 4

Rotate piece 90° clockwise.
Row 1 Ch 2, working into side of each row, work 1 ex-sc in side of next 56 rows, change to A, fasten off C, turn.
Rows 2 and 3 Rep rows 5 and 6 of section 1 (56 sts).
Rows 4–19 Rep rows 3–6 of section 1. Change to C at end of row 19 and do not turn. Fasten off A and B.

SECTION 5

Rotate piece 90° clockwise.
Row 1 Ch 2, working into side of each row, work 1 ex-sc in side of next 18 rows; work next set of sts into starting chain as foll: work 1 ex-sc in next 20 ch; work 1 ex-sc into side of next 19 rows, change to A, fasten off C, turn.
Rows 2 and 3 Rep rows 5 and 6 of section 1 (57 sts).
Rows 4–27 Rep rows 3–6 of section 1. Change to C at end of row 27 and do not turn. Leave A and B attached.

BORDER

Rnd 1 Ch 2, [work 1 ex-sc into side of each row and into each ex-sc to corner, (ex-sc, ch 1, ex-sc) into corner, rotate piece 90°] 4 times. change to A, join with sl st to 2nd ch of beg ch-2, turn.
Rnd 2 Ch 2, 1 ex-sc in next st, [(ex-sc, ch 1, ex-sc) in ch-sp, 1 ex-sc in each st to next ch-sp] 3 times, (ex-sc, ch 1, ex-sc) in next ch-sp, 1 ex-sc in each st to end, change to B, join with sl st to 2nd ch of beg ch-2, turn.
Rnd 3 Ch 2, [1 ex-sc in each st to next ch-sp, (ex-sc, ch 1, ex-sc) in next ch-sp] 4 times, 1 ex-sc in each st to end, change to A, join with sl st to beg ch-2, turn.
Rnd 4 Rep rnd 2, do not change color at end of rnd, turn.
Rnd 5 Ch 1, 1 sl st in each st. Fasten off.

PLACEMENT DIAGRAM

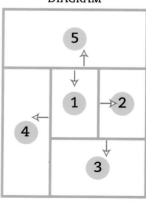

← = Direction of work

Ducks IN A ROW

YOU'LL NEED

YARN: 🔟 14oz/400g, 970yd/890m of any DK weight wool in ecru (MC)

12¼oz/250g, 850yd/780m in blue (A)

8¾oz/150g, 610yd/560m in yellow (B)

1¾oz/50g, 120yd/110m in orange (C)

HOOK: Size E/4 (3.5mm) crochet hook *or size to obtain gauge*

ADDITIONAL: 1 skein embroidery floss in black, yarn needle

FINISHED MEASUREMENTS

Approx 33"x 41½"/84cm x 106cm

Each dc block approx 8"x 8"/20.5cm x 20.5cm

GAUGE

18 sts and 9½ rows to 4"/10cm over dc using size E/4 (3.5mm) crochet hook.

Take time to check gauge.

NOTES

1 Intarsia color blocks are worked with separate balls of yarn or bobbins. The yarns are not carried across or worked over by new colors.

2 Join new color by working st in old color to last 2 lps; leaving 6"/15cm tail, complete st by drawing new color through 2 lps and continue with new color.

STITCH GLOSSARY

BL Work through back loop only.

Dc2tog (over 2 sts) [Yo and draw lp in next st, yo and draw through 2 lps] twice, yo and draw through all 3 lps.

SOLID SQUARES

(make 6 blue and 6 white)

Ch 38.

Row 1 Work 1 dc in 4th ch from hook (ch 3 counts as 1 dc), 1 dc in each ch across—36 dc. Turn.

Row 2 Ch 3 (counts as 1 dc), skip first dc, 1 dc in each dc across, end with dc in top of ch-3. Turn.

Rep row 2 until square measures approx 8"/20.5cm. Fasten off.

DUCK SQUARE

(make 8)

DUCK

With MC, ch 37. Work duck chart 1 as foll:

Row 1 (RS) Work 1 sc in 2nd ch from the hook and in next 9 ch; with B, 1 sc in next 18 ch; with MC, 1 sc in last 8 ch. Turn.

Rows 2–30 Ch 1, sc in each sc and foll Chart I for duck motif. Fasten off.

WATER

With A, ch 39.

Row 1 Inserting hook under "V" of lps, 1 dc in 4th ch, *1 dc in each of next 3 ch, [dc2tog over next 2 ch] twice, 1 dc in each of next 3 ch, [2 dc in next ch] twice; rep from *, ending last rep with [2 dc in next ch] once. The back lps form the waves of the water. Turn.

Row 2 Ch 3 (counts as 1 dc) and work in BL only, 1 dc in first st, *1 dc in each of next 3 sts, [dc2tog over next 2 sts] twice, 1 dc in each of next 3 sts, [2 dc in next st] twice; rep from *, ending last rep with 2 dc in last st. Turn.

Rows 3–5 Rep row 2.

Row 6 Ch 1, 1 sc in each st across. Turn.

Row 7 Ch 1, 1 sc in each st across. Fasten off. This edge is the bottom of the duck square.

WING

With B, ch 3. Join with sl st to form ring.

Rnd 1 Ch 2, 7 hdc in ring. Join with sl st to top of beg ch-2.

Rnd 2 Ch 3, 2 hdc in joining sp, sl st in next st. Fasten off.

FINISHING

ASSEMBLING DUCK SQUARES

With wave edge upward, position against bottom edge of duck motif so that length of block measures approx 8"/20.5cm. Sew water to front of duck in backstitch, then hem edge to back of water. Embroider face on each duck. Tack wing to side of duck.

EDGINGS

With C, sc evenly around each solid and duck square, with 3 sc in each corner. Fasten off.

Arrange squares according to Chart II and sew together.

Rnd 1 With C, sc evenly around entire blanket, with 3 sc in each corner. Join with sl st to first sc.

Rnd 2 With C, ch 1, *working from left to right, 1 sc in next st to right, ch 1, skip 1; rep from * around. Join with sl st to first sc. Fasten off.

Weave in all ends and block.

Jack Deutsch

Color Key

☐ Ecru (MC)

▨ Yellow (B)

Stitch Key

● Attach Wing

— Straight Stitch

● Eye

▬ Straight Stitch

CHART II

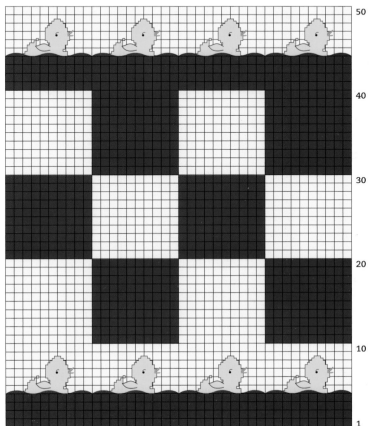

CHART I

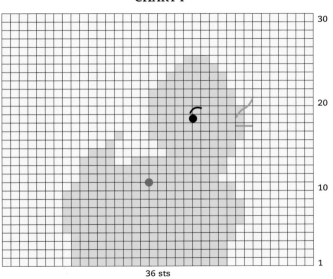

36 sts

Connect THE DOTS

YOU'LL NEED

YARN:  3½oz/100g, 220yd/200m of any worsted weight cotton/acrylic blend in pale gray (A)

1¾oz/50g, 110yd/100m in magenta (B), medium blue (C), cherry red (D), brown (E), brick red (F), yellow (G), gold (H), royal blue (I), pale orange (J), and lavender (K)

HOOK: Size E/4 (3.5mm) crochet hook *or size to obtain gauge.*

FINISHED MEASUREMENTS

Approx 33" x 33"/83.5cm x 83.5cm

GAUGE

1 medallion to 5"/12.5cm using size E/4 (3.5mm) crochet hook.
Take time to check gauge.

NOTES

1 Colors are used randomly and can be placed as desired OR use the placement diagram which shows the color sequence of each square as shown in the photo.
2 When changing colors for each rnd, dc over yarn tails to hide and then cut. This eliminates weaving in all the tails.

MEDALLION MOTIF

Make 49 medallions.
Ch 5, sl st in first ch to form ring.
Rnd 1 Ch 3 (counts as dc), work 19 dc in ring, end with sl st in 3rd ch of beg ch-3—20 dc. Fasten off.
Rnd 2 Join new color with sl st into next dc, ch 1, sc in same st, ch 3 (counts as dc, ch 1), dc, ch 1 in each dc around, end with sl st in 2nd ch of beg ch 3—20 dc and 20 ch-1 sps. Fasten off.
Rnd 3 Join new color with sl st in ch 1 sp, ch 1, (sc, ch 2, dc) all in same sp, 2 dc in each ch-1 sp around, end with sl st in 2nd ch of beg ch-2—40 dc. Fasten off.
Rnd 4 Join new color with sl st in next dc, (ch 1, sc, ch 2) in same st, *2 dc in next st, dc in next st; rep from * around, end with sl st in 2nd ch of beg ch-2—60 dc. Fasten off.

FINISHING

Block medallions to measurement.

JOINING MEDALLIONS

Arrange medallions with right sides facing 7 across and 7 down as shown in placement diagram. With A, sc medallions together using back loops only of each medallion as indicated below. Working from right to left and starting at the lower right corner, sc in the back loops of the top and bottom circles tog over 5 sts. Sc in the back loop only of the top circle only over 5 sts. Then sc the next bottom circle to the top circle in the back loop only over 5 sts. Sc in the back loop only of the second bottom circle over 5 sts. Then sc second bottom circle to second top circle over 5 sts. Cont sc over 5 sts of the top circle. Sc 3rd bottom circle to 2nd top circle over 5 sts.
Then sc in bottom circle only for 5 sts. Cont across row in this way to end and fasten off. Rep for the next 5 rows. Turn work and rep pattern. Use sl st (5 sl sts) over previous sc seam. Do not fasten off after last seam at edge.

EDGING

Rnd 1 After seaming the last row, cont with A and ch 1, sc in each dc around entire blanket.
Note For each circle do 2 incs (2 sc in st) evenly spaced. This prevents the circle from rolling in. For each corner circle do 3 incs evenly spaced. Sl st over seams between circles. End with sl st in ch 1 at beg of rnd.

PLACEMENT DIAGRAM

COLOR KEY
A Mint
B Magenta
C Teal
D Tangerine
E Olive
F Brick
G Maize
H Wheat
I Turquoise
J Salmon
K Lavender

Row 1: B,J,K,I — I,G,B,C — G,E,I,D — I,J,K,B — B,K,E,G — B,I,H,F — J,B,K,D

Row 2: G,D,F,E — G,F,J,B — K,J,G,C — G,D,J,K — B,J,C,E — H,G,B,I — I,K,J,F

Row 3: D,C,E,B — E,G,D,K — D,G,B,E — G,C,H,I — K,G,I,J — E,G,F,D — F,K,B,C

Row 4: J,D,C,F — C,I,J,D — D,E,G,F — D,J,F,G — C,B,G,K — I,C,H,G — I,F,K,E

Row 5: I,J,D,H — E,H,F,J — G,K,I,H — G,E,D,J — B,C,G,D — H,B,F,C — E,G,F,H

Row 6: C,H,E,K — G,B,E,F — D,E,J,C — E,D,G,I — I,J,C,K — B,C,K,J — B,I,H,K

Row 7: J,I,D,C — K,C,B,H — F,E,I,B — K,J,H,E — K,I,G,B — F,J,E,H — D,B,J,I

Bunny HOP

YOU'LL NEED

YARN:  24oz/690g, 1500yd/1375m of any worsted weight variegated wool (MC)

1¾oz/50g, 110yd/100m in pale pink (CC)

1yd/1m black worsted weight yarn

HOOK: Size J/10 (6mm) crochet hook *or size to obtain gauge*

ADDITIONAL: Polyester fiberfill, Yarn needle

FINISHED MEASUREMENTS

Approx 34"x 34"/86.5cm x 86.5cm

GAUGE

14 sts and 9 rows to 4"/10cm over pat using size J/10 (6mm) crochet hook. *Take time to check gauge.*

STITCH GLOSSARY

Sc2tog (over 2 sts) [Draw lp in next st] twice, yo and draw through all 3 lps.
BL Back loop
FL Front loop

BUNNY

HEAD

Note Worked in spiral—do not join rnds. Mark first st of each rnd.
With MC, ch 2.
Rnd 1 6 sc in 2nd ch from hook—6 sc.
Rnd 2 2 sc in each st around—12 sc.
Rnd 3 *1 sc in next st, 2 sc in next st; rep from * around—18 sc.
Rnds 4–6 1 sc in each st around—18 sc.
Rnd 7 In BL only, *1 sc in each of next 2 sts, 2 sc in next st; rep from * around—24 sc.
Rnd 8 *1 sc in each of next 3 sts, 2 sc in next st; rep from * around—30 sc.
Rnd 9 *1 sc in each of next 4 sts, 2 sc in next st; rep from * around—36 sc.
Rnd 10 *1 sc in each of next 5 sts, 2 sc in next st; rep from * around—42 sc.
Rnd 11 *1 sc in each of next 6 sts, 2 sc in next st; rep from * around—48 sc.
Rnds 12–15 1 sc in each st around—48 sc.

Rnd 16 *1 sc in each of next 6 sts, sc2tog; rep from * around—42 sc.
Rnd 17 *1 sc in each of next 5 sts, sc2tog; rep from * around—36 sc.
Rnd 18 *1 sc in each of next 4 sts, sc2tog; rep from * around—30 sc.
Rnd 19 *1 sc in each of next 3 sts, sc2tog; rep from * around—24 sc. Mark rnd.
Rnd 20 In BL only, *1 sc in each of next 2 sts, sc2tog; rep from * around—18 sc. Stuff with fiberfill.
Rnd 21 *1 sc in next st, sc2tog; rep from * around—12 sc.
Rnd 22 Sc2tog around—6 sc.
Stuff to complete. Sew to close.

EARS (make 2)

Note Join at the end of each rnd. You will alternate starting rounds with MC and CC.
With MC, ch 2.
Rnd 1 6 sc in 2nd ch from hook. Join CC (do not cut MC)—6 sts. Join with sl st to first sc. Turn.
Rnd 2 With CC, ch 1, 1 sc in next st, 2 sc in next st; with MC, *1 sc in next st, 2 sc in next st; rep from * around—3CC and 6MC sts. Join with sl st to first sc. Turn.
Rnd 3 With MC, ch 1, 1 sc in each of next 2 sts, 2 sc in next st, 1 sc in each of next 2 sts; with CC, 2 sc in next st, 1 sc in each of next 2 sts, 2 sc in last st—6 CC and 6 MC sts. Join with sl st to first sc. Turn.
Rnd 4 With CC, ch 1, 1 sc in each of next 3 sts, 2 sc in next st, 1 sc in each of next 2 sts; with MC, 1 sc in next st, 2 sc in next st, 1 sc in each of next 3 sts, 2 sc in last st—7 CC and 8 MC sts. Join with sl st to first sc. Turn.
Rnd 5 With MC, ch 1, 1 sc in each of next 4 sts, 2 sc in next st, 1 sc in each of next 3 sts; with CC, 1 sc in next st, 2 sc in next st, 1 sc in each of next 4 sts, 2 sc in last st—9 CC and 9 MC sts. Join with sl st to first sc. Turn.
Rnd 6 With CC, ch 1, 1 sc in each of next 9 sts; with MC, 1 sc in each of next 9 sts—9 CC and 9 MC sts. Join with sl st to first sc. Turn.
Rnd 7 With MC, ch 1, 1 sc in each of next 9 sts; with CC, 1 sc in each of next 9 sts—9 CC and 9 MC sts. Join with sl st to first sc. Turn.
Rnds 8–23 Rep rnds 6 and 7.

Rnd 24 With CC, ch 1, [1 sc in next st, sc2tog] 3 times; with MC, [1 sc in next st, sc2tog] 3 times—6 CC and 6 MC sts. Join with sl st to first sc. Turn.
Rnd 25 With MC, ch 1, sc2tog around. Join with sl st to first sc.
Fasten off, leaving 10"/25.5cm tail for sewing.

BLANKET

With MC, ch 54. Connect bunny head by working through FL of rnd 19 of head; flatten round to work through two sts at a time (start with first and last sts tog), 1 sc in each of next 9 sts, ch 54.
Row 1 Skip 2 ch (counts as 1 sc), (1 hdc, 1 dc) in next ch, *skip 2 ch, (1 sc, 1 hdc, 1 dc) in next ch; rep from * across to last 3 ch, skip 2 ch, 1 sc in last ch (the sc connecting the head counts as ch st). Turn.
Row 2 Ch 1, (1 hdc, 1 dc) in first sc, *skip (1 dc, 1 hdc), (1 sc, 1 hdc, 1 dc) in next sc; rep from * to last 3 sts, skip (1 dc, 1 hdc), 1 sc in top of t-ch. Turn.
Rows 3–77 Rep row 2 until blanket measures 34"/86.5cm from beg. Fasten off.

FINISHING

Weave in ends.

EARS

Flatten and sew, with pink side toward head, to sides near top between rnds 14 and 17.

EMBROIDERY

With CC, embroider nose with satin stitch starting at center of face over rnds 2 and 3. With CC, embroider mouth with straight stitch from bottom of nose and near rnd 2. With black, embroider eyes with satin stitch starting on rnd 7, working over rnds 7 and 8 and near center with 1 to 2 sts in between eyes.

Darling BLOCKS

YOU'LL NEED

YARN:  7oz/200g, 370yd/340m of any worsted weight wool in grey (A), pink (B), lime green (C), and blue (D)

HOOK: Size N/15 (10mm) crochet hook *or size to obtain gauge*

FINISHED MEASUREMENTS

Approx 21½" x 28"/54.5 x 71cm

GAUGE

One square to 4¼"/11cm using size N/15 (10mm) crochet hook with 2 strands of yarn held tog (before felting).
Take time to check gauge.

NOTE

Use 2 strands of yarn held tog throughout.

SQUARE

(make 63)
With 2 strands of A held tog, ch 4. Join ch with a sl st forming a ring.
Rnd 1 (RS) Ch 3 (counts as 1 dc), work 2 dc in ring, [ch 3, work 3 dc in ring] 3 times, ch 3, join rnd with a sl st in top of beg ch-3.
Rnd 2 Ch 4 (counts as 1 dc and ch 1), [work (3 dc, ch 3, 3 dc) in next ch-3 sp, ch 1] 3 times, work (3 dc, ch 3, 2 dc) in last ch-3 sp, join rnd with a sl st in 3rd ch of beg ch-4. Fasten off. Make 15 squares more using A, 16 each using B and C, and 15 using D.

FINISHING

Using A and working in back lps, whipstitch squares tog foll placement diagram.

EDGING

With RS facing, join 2 strands of B with a sl st in any corner ch-3 sp.
Rnd 1 (RS) Ch 1, work 3 sc in same sp as joining, sc in each st around, working 3 sc in each ch-3 corner sp, join rnd with a sl st in first sc. Fasten off.

FELTING

Place blanket in a zippered pillowcase and put into washing machine. Use hot-water wash, a regular (not delicate) cycle and lowest water level. Add a tablespoon of laundry detergent and an old pair of jeans for agitation. Check piece every 5–10 minutes, agitating until stitches are not seen and piece measures 21½" x 28"/54.5 x 71cm. Rinse in cold water; do not allow to go through spin cycle. Remove from pillowcase, then gently roll in towels to assist in drying if blanket is extremely wet. Hand-block to measurements. Let air dry flat for 1 to 2 days.

Jack Deutsch

PLACEMENT DIAGRAM

A	D	C	B	A	D	C
B	A	D	C	B	A	D
C	B	A	D	C	B	A
D	C	B	A	D	C	B
A	D	C	B	A	D	C
B	A	D	C	B	A	D
C	B	A	D	C	B	A
D	C	B	A	D	C	B
C	B	A	D	C	B	A

Sugarplum FAIRIES

Jack Deutsch

YOU'LL NEED

YARN:  8¾oz/150g, 625yd/575m of any worsted weight wool in light purple (MC)

1¾oz/50g, 125yd/114m in magenta (CC)

HOOK: Size H/8 (5mm) crochet hook *or size to obtain gauge*

ADDITIONAL: Yarn needle

FINISHED MEASUREMENTS

Approx 25"x 31"/63.5cm x 79cm

GAUGE

16 sts and 8 rows to 4"/10cm over iris st pat using size H/8 (5mm) crochet hook.
Take time to check gauge.

BLANKET

With MC, ch 95.
Row 1 (2 dc, ch 1, 2 dc) in 5th ch from hook, *skip 3 ch, (2 dc, ch 1, 2 dc) in next ch; rep from * to last 2 ch, skip 1 ch, 1 dc in last ch. Turn.

Row 2 Ch 3, skip first 3 dc, *(2 dc, ch 1, 2 dc) in ch-1 sp, skip next 4 dc; rep from * ending with skip last 2 dc, 1 dc in last ch. Turn.
Rep row 2 until piece measures 29"/73.5cm from beg. Fasten off.

EDGING

Rnd 1 (RS) With CC, ch 1, 1 sc in each st or space around blanket. Join with sl st to beg ch-1. Turn.
Rnd 2 Ch 1, skip first sc, 1 sc in each sc around. Join with 1 sc to beg ch-1. Turn.
Rnd 3 Ch 1, skip first sc, *skip 1 sc, 5 dc in next sc, skip 1 sc, 1 sc in next sc; rep from * around. Join with 1 sc to beg ch-1. Fasten off.

FINISHING

Weave in ends.

Creamsicle COVERLET

FINISHED MEASUREMENTS

Approx 34"x 34"/86.4cm x 86.4cm

GAUGE

18 sts and 11 rows to 4"/10cm in dc using size H/8 (5mm) crochet hook.
Take time to check gauge.

STITCH GLOSSARY

Corner (2 Dc, ch 3, 2 dc) in ch sp.
Fan (3 Dc, ch 1, 3 dc) in ch-1 sp of V-St.
V-St (1 Hdc, ch 1, 1 hdc) in same st.
Back Crossed DC (BCdc) (over 2 sps) Skip ch sp, 1 dc in next ch sp, working behind last dc made, 1 dc in skipped ch sp. Shell (5 Dc) in same st.

BLANKET

CENTER MOTIF

With MC and size H/8 (5mm) hook, ch 8. Join with sl st to first ch to form ring.
Rnd 1 Ch 1, 16 sc in ring. Join with sl st to first sc—16 sc.
Rnd 2 Ch 1, 1 sc in same sp, *ch 7, skip 3 sts, 1 sc; rep from *, ending last rep with skip 3 sts—4 ch-7 sp. Join with sl st to first sc.
Rnd 3 Sl st across to 3rd ch of first ch sp, ch 3 (counts as 1 dc), 1 dc in same ch, *ch 2, 2 dc, ch 3 in first ch sp, dc2tog (inserting hook into first ch-7 sp for 1st leg and into second ch-7 sp for 2nd leg), ch 3, 2 dc in second ch-7 sp; rep from * around, ending last rep with dc2tog, ch 3. Join with sl st to top of beg ch-3.
Rnd 4 Sl st in next dc and next ch, ch 3 (counts as 1 dc), 1 dc in same ch, *ch 3, 2 dc in ch-3 sp, ch 3, skip 2 sts, 3 dc in next

ch-3 sp, 1 dc in top of dc2tog, 3 dc in next ch-3 sp, ch 3, skip 2 sts, 2 dc in next ch sp; rep from *, ending last rep with ch 3, skip 2 sts. Join with sl st to top of beg ch-3.
Rnd 5 Sl st in next dc and next ch, ch 3, 2 dc in ch, *ch 3, 3 dc in first ch sp, ch 6, skip (2 dc, ch 3, 2 dc), 1 dc in each of next 5 dc, ch 6, skip (1 dc, ch 3, 2 dc), 3 dc in next ch-3 sp; rep from *, ending last rep with ch 6, skip (1 dc, ch 3, 2 dc). Join with sl st to top of beg ch-3.
Rnd 6 Ch 3 (counts as 1 dc), 1 dc in each of next 2 dc, *(3 dc, ch 5, 3 dc) in first ch sp, 1 dc in each of next 3 dc, ch 6, skip ch-6 sp and 1 dc, 1 dc in each of next 3 dc, ch 6, skip 1 dc and ch-6 sp, 1 dc in each of next 3 dc; rep from *, ending last rep skip 1 dc and ch-6 sp. Join with sl st to top of beg ch-3.
Rnd 7 Ch 3 (counts as 1 dc), skip 1 dc, 1 dc in each of the next 5 dc, *work Corner, 1 dc in each of next 6 dc, 6 dc in ch-6 sp, 1 dc in each of next 3 dc, 6 dc in ch-6 sp, 1 dc in each of next 6 dc; rep from *, ending last rep with 6 dc in ch-6 sp. Join with sl st to top of beg ch-3—136 sts. Fasten off.

FAN STITCH BAND

Rnd 8 Join CC to next dc and ch 3 (count as 1 dc), (2 dc, ch 1, 3 dc) in same st, *skip 3 dc, 1 sc in each of next 2 dc, Corner in ch sp, 1 sc in each of next 2 dc, skip 3, [(3 dc, ch 1, 3 dc) in next st, skip 3 dc, 1 sc, ch 1, skip 1, 1 sc, skip 3] twice, (3 dc, ch 1, 3 dc) in next st; rep from *, ending last rep with [(3 dc, ch 1, 3 dc) in next st, skip 3 dc, 1 sc, ch 1, skip 1, 1 sc, skip 3] twice. Join with sl st to top of beg ch-3.
Rnd 9 Ch 3, skip 3 dc, *1 sc in ch sp of Fan, ch 3, skip 3 dc and 1 sc, V-St in next sc, 1 dc in each of next 2 sts, Corner in ch sp, 1 dc in each of next 2 dc, V-St in next st, [ch 3, skip 1 sc and 3 dc, 1 sc in ch sp of Fan, ch 3, skip 3 dc and 1 sc, V-St in ch sp] twice, ch 3; rep from *, ending last rep with skip 1. Join with sl st to base of beg ch-3.
Rnd 10 Ch 3, 1 sc in 3 ch sp, ch 1, skip 1 sc, 1 sc in ch-3 sp, *Fan in next ch-1 sp, skip 3, 1 sc in each of next 2 dc, Corner in ch sp, 1 sc in each of next 2 sts, skip 3, [Fan in ch-1 sp, 1 sc in next ch-3 sp, skip 1 sc, ch 1, 1 sc in next ch-3 sp] 3 times; rep from *, ending last rep with (3 dc, ch

1, 2 dc) in ch-1 sp. Join with sl st to top of beg ch-3.
Rnd 11 2 Sl st, ch 3 (counts as 1 hdc and ch 1), 1 hdc in sl st, ch 3, skip 3 dc, 1 sc in ch sp of Fan, *ch 3, skip 3 dc and 1 sc, V-St in next sc, 1 dc in each of next 2 sts, Corner in ch sp, 1 dc in each of next 2 sts, V-St in next st, [ch 3, skip 1 sc and 3 dc, 1 sc in ch sp of Fan, ch 3, skip 3 dc and 1 sc, V-St in ch sp] twice, ch 3, skip 1 sc and 3 dc, 1 sc in ch sp of Fan; rep from *, ending last rep with ch 3. Join with sl st in 2nd ch of beg ch-3.
Rnd 12 Ch 3, (2 dc, ch 1, 3 dc) in ch-1 sp, 1 sc in ch-3 sp, skip 1 sc, 1 sc in ch-3 sp, Fan in ch-1 sp, *skip 3, 1 sc in each of next 2 sts, Corner in ch sp, 1 sc in each of next 2 sts, skip 3, [Fan, 1 sc in ch-3 sp, skip 1, ch 1, 1 sc in ch-3 sp] 4 times, Fan in next ch-1 sp; rep from *, ending last rep with [Fan, 1 sc in ch-3 sp, skip 1, ch 1, 1 sc in ch-3 sp] 3 times. Join with sl st to top of beg ch-3.
Rnd 13 Ch 3, 1 sc in ch sp of Fan, ch 3, V-St in ch-1 sp, ch 3, 1 sc in ch sp of Fan, *ch 3, skip 3 dc and 1 sc, V-St in next sc, 1 dc in each of next 2 sts, Corner in ch sp, 1 dc in each of next 2 sts, V-St in next st, ch 3, 1 sc in ch sp of Fan, [ch 3, V-St in ch-1 sp, ch 3, 1 sc in ch sp of Fan] 4 times; rep from *, ending last rep with [ch 3, V-St in ch-1 sp, ch 3, 1 sc in ch sp of Fan] twice, ch 3, V-St in ch-1 sp. Join with sl st to base of beg ch-3.
Rnd 14 Ch 3, [1 sc in ch-3 sp, skip 1 sc, 1 sc in ch-3 sp, Fan in ch sp] twice, *skip 3, 1 sc in each of next 2 dc, Corner in ch sp, 2 sc, skip 3, [Fan in ch-1 sp, 1 sc in next ch-3 sp, skip 1 sc, ch 1, 1 sc in next ch-3 sp] 5 times, Fan in ch-1 sp; rep from *, ending last rep with [Fan, 1 sc in ch-3 sp, skip 1, ch 1, 1 sc in ch-3 sp] 3 times. Join with sl st to top of beg ch-3.
Rnd 15 2 Sl st, ch 3 (counts as 1 hdc and ch 1), 1 hdc in ch sp, ch 3, 1 sc in ch sp of Fan, ch 3, V-St in ch-1 sp, ch 3, 1 sc in ch sp of Fan, *ch 3, skip 3 dc and 1 sc, V-St in next sc, 1 dc in each of next 2 sts, Corner in ch sp, 1 dc in each of next 2 sts, V-St in next st, [ch 3, 1 sc in ch sp of Fan, ch 3, V-St in ch sp] 5 times, ch 3, 1 sc in ch sp of Fan; rep from *, ending last rep with [ch 3, 1 sc in ch sp of Fan, ch 3, V-St in ch sp] 3 times, ch 3, 1 sc in ch sp of Fan, ch

3. Join with sl st in 2nd ch of beg ch-3.

Rnds 16–18 Rep rnds 12–14 increasing number of st reps between [ ] as established by 1 on each rnd—352 sts.

Rnd 19 2 Sl st, ch 5, (counts as 1 hdc and ch 3), [1 sc in ch sp of Fan, ch 3, 1 hdc in next ch-1 sp, ch 3] 3 times, *1 sc in ch sp of Fan, ch 3, skip 3 dc and 1 sc,1 hdc in each of next 4 sts, Corner in ch sp, 1 hdc in each of next 4 sts, [ch 3, 1 sc in ch sp of Fan, ch 3, 1 hdc in next ch-1 sp] 7 times, ch 3; rep from *, ending last rep with [ch 3, 1 sc in Fan sp, ch 3, 1 hdc in next ch-1 sp] 4 times, ch 3. Join with sl st in 2nd ch of beg ch-5—316 sts.

Rnd 20 Ch 3 (counts as 1 dc), [3 dc in ch-3 sp, 1 dc in sc, 3 dc in ch-3 sp, 1 dc in hdc] 3 times, *6 dc, Corner in ch sp, 6 dc, [3 dc in ch sp, 1 dc in sc, 3 dc in ch-3 sp, 1 dc in hdc] 8 times; rep from *, ending last rep with [3 dc in ch sp, 1 dc in sc, 3 dc in ch-3 sp, 1 dc in hdc] 4 times, 3 dc in ch sp, 1 dc in sc, 3 dc in ch-3 sp. Join with sl st to top of beg ch-3—332 dc and ch-3 corner sts.

EYELET BAND

Rnd 21 Ch 4 (count as 1 dc and ch 1), [skip 1, 1 dc, ch 1] 15 times, *(1 dc, ch 1) 3 times in corner ch, 1 dc in first st, ch 1, [skip 1, 1 dc, ch 1] 39 times; rep from *, ending last rep with [skip 1, 1 dc, ch 1] 23 times. Join with sl st in 3rd ch of beg ch-4.

Rnd 22 Ch 3 (do not count), *BCdc over next 2 ch sps; rep from *, ending last rep with 1 dc in ch sp of beg ch-3, 1 dc in last ch of rnd behind previous st. Join with sl st to top of beg ch-3.

Rnd 23 Ch 4 (count as 1 dc and ch 1), [skip 1, 1 dc, ch 1] 15 times,*(1 dc, ch 1) in each of next 4 corner sts, [skip 1, 1 dc, ch 1] 41 times; rep from *, ending last rep [skip 1, 1 dc, ch 1] 25 times. Join with sl st to 3rd ch of beg ch-4.

Rnd 24 Ch 3 (count as 1 dc), [1 dc in ch, 1 dc in dc] 16 times, *ch 3 for corner, [1 dc in ch, 1 dc in dc] 45 times; rep from *, ending last rep with [1 dc in ch, 1 dc in dc] 28 times, 1 dc in ch. Join with sl st to top of beg ch-3—372 dc and corner ch-3 sts. Fasten off.

SHELL BAND

With RS facing and size H/8 (5mm) hook, attach MC in 51st st from right hand corner (do not count corner ch sts).

Rnd 25 Ch 3 (count as 1 dc), 2 dc in same st, [skip 2, 1 sc in next st, ch 5, skip 5, 1 sc in next st, skip 2, Shell in next st] 3 times, skip 2, *1 sc, ch 5, skip corner sp, 1 sc in next st, [skip 2, Shell in next st, skip 2, 1 sc in next st, ch 5, skip 5, 1 sc in next st] 7 times, skip 2, 5 dc in next st, skip 2, 1 sc in next st; rep from *, ending last rep with [skip 2, Shell in next st, skip 2, 1 sc in next st, ch 5, skip 5, 1 sc in next st] 4 times, skip 2, 2 dc in beg ch-3 sp. Join with sl st to top of beg ch-3.

Rnd 26 Ch 5, 1 sc in 5 ch sp, [ch 5, 1 sc in 3rd dc of Shell, ch 5, 1 sc in next ch sp] 3 times, *ch 5, 1 sc in same ch sp, [ch 5, 1 sc in 3rd dc of Shell, ch 5, 1 sc in next ch sp] 8 times, rep from *, ending last rep with [ch 5, 1 sc in 3rd dc of Shell, ch 5, 1 sc in next ch sp] 4 times, ch 5. Join with sl st to 1st ch of beg ch-5.

Rnd 27 [Ch 5, 1 sc in ch sp, Shell in next sc, 1 sc in ch-5 sp] 4 times, *ch 5, 1 sc in same ch sp, [Shell in next sc, 1 sc in ch-5 sp, ch 5, 1 sc in ch sp] 9 times; rep from *, ending last rep with [Shell in next sc, 1 sc in ch-5 sp, ch 5, 1 sc in ch sp] 5 times. Join with sl st to 1st ch of beg ch-5.

Rnd 28 [Ch 5, 1 sc in 3rd dc of Shell, ch 5, 1 sc in ch sp] 4 times *ch 5, 1 sc in same ch sp, [ch 5, 1 sc in 3rd dc of Shell, ch 5, 1 sc in ch sp] 9 times; rep from *, ending last rep with [ch 5, 1 sc in 3rd dc of Shell, ch 5, 1 sc in ch sp] 5 times. Join with 1 sc in base ch of beg ch-5.

Rnd 29 Ch 3 (counts as 1 dc), 2 dc in same st, 1 sc in ch sp, ch 5, 1 sc in next ch sp, [Shell in next sc, 1 sc in next ch sp, ch 5, 1 sc in next ch sp] 3 times, *Shell in next sc, 1 sc in next ch sp, ch 5, 1 sc in same ch sp, [Shell in next sc, 1 sc in next ch sp, ch 5, 1 sc in next ch sp] 9 times; rep from *, ending last rep with [Shell in next sc, 1 sc in next ch sp, ch 5, 1 sc in next ch sp] 5 times, 2 dc in same st as beg ch-3. Join with sl st to 2nd ch of beg ch-3.

Rnd 30 [Ch 5, 1 sc in ch sp, ch 5, 1 sc in 3rd dc of Shell] 3 times, *ch 5, 1 sc in next ch sp, ch 5, 1 sc in same ch sp, [ch 5, 1 sc in 3rd dc of Shell, 1 sc in next ch sp, ch 5] 8 times; rep from *, ending last rep with [ch 5, 1 sc in 3rd dc of Shell, 1 sc in next ch sp, ch 5] 5 times. Join with 1 sc in base of ch-5.

Rnds 31–41 Rep rnds 27–30 twice, then rnds 27–29 once, increasing number of st reps between [ ] as established on each rnd.

Rnd 42 Ch 3, 1 sc in ch-5 sp [ch 3, 1 sc in 3rd dc of Shell, ch 3, 1 sc in next ch sp] 6 times, *ch 3, 1 sc in same ch sp, [ch 3, 1 sc in 3rd dc of Shell, ch 3, 1 sc in next ch sp] 14 times, rep from *, ending last rep with [ch 3, 1 sc in 3rd dc of Shell, ch 3, 1 sc in next ch sp] 7 times, ch 3, 1 sc in 3rd dc of Shell. Join with sl st to 1st ch of beg ch-3.

Rnd 43 Ch 3 (count as 1 dc), skip 1 sc, 3 dc in ch sp, [1 dc in sc, 3 dc in ch sp] 12 times, *1 dc in sc, (2 dc, ch 3, 2 dc) in corner ch, [1 dc in sc, 3 dc in ch sp] 28 times; rep from *, ending last rep with [1 dc in sc, 3 dc in ch sp] 15 times—480 sts. Join with sl st to top of beg ch-3.

EYELET BAND

Rnds 44–47 Rep rnds 21–24, increasing number of st reps between [ ] as established on each rnd—512 sts. Fasten off.

RUFFLE

Rnd 48 With CC, 1 sc in each st around. Change to size G/6 (4mm) hook.

Rnd 49 Ch 3 (count as 1 sc and ch 2), skip 1 sc, *1 sc in next sc, ch 2, skip 1 sc; rep from * around. Join with sl st to 1st ch of beg ch-3.

Rnds 50–52 Ch 5 (count as 1 hdc and ch 3), *1 hdc in next hdc, ch 3; rep from * around. Join with sl st to 2nd ch of beg ch-5.

Rnd 53 Ch 6 (count as 1 hdc and ch 4), *1 hdc in next hdc, ch 4; rep from * around. Join with sl st to 2nd ch beg ch-6.

Rnd 54 Ch 7 (count as 1 hdc and ch 5), *1 hdc in next hdc, ch 5; rep from * around. Join with sl st to 2nd ch st of beg ch-7.

Rnd 55 Ch 8 (count as 1 sc and ch 7), *1 sc in next hdc, ch 7; rep from * around. Join with sl st to 1st ch st of beg ch-8. Fasten off.

FINISHING

Weave in loose ends. Steam lightly, pulling slightly to open Shell lace and pulling ruffle into points. Let dry. Thread ribbon through eyelet rows and tie into bows at corners as shown.